Introduction to Microsoft Teams

The User's Guide to Efficient Collaboration

Dr. Patrick Jones

OLYMPUS ACADEMY
PRESS

The Microsoft Teams Companion Series

The Microsoft Teams Companion Series

Welcome to *The Microsoft Teams Companion Series*—your step-by-step guide to mastering every aspect of Microsoft Teams. Each book in this collection covers a distinct area, ensuring that by the end, you'll possess an in-depth, holistic understanding of Teams for personal use, business, education, or enterprise-level deployments.

Here's what you'll find in this series:

1. *Introduction to Microsoft Teams*
2. *Teams & Channels*
3. *Chats & Meetings*
4. *Teams Phones*
5. *Apps & Integrations*
6. *Copilot in Microsoft Teams*
7. *Accessibility in Microsoft Teams*
8. *Microsoft Teams in Education*
9. *Security, Compliance, and Administration in Microsoft Teams*
10. *Expert Tips & Troubleshooting: Becoming a Microsoft Teams Power User*

Looking to dive even deeper into the Microsoft ecosystem? Explore our other companion series—*The Microsoft 365 Companion Series, The Microsoft Intune Companion Series, and The Microsoft Purview Companion Series*—all available on Amazon. Each provides the same clear, comprehensive coverage you'll find here, helping you expand and refine your skills across the full spectrum of Microsoft products and services.

TABLE OF CONTENTS

CHAPTER 1: WHY MICROSOFT TEAMS?

Modern workplaces thrive on fast, efficient communication. But as email inboxes overflow and employees juggle multiple apps for chatting, file sharing, and video calls, confusion and inefficiency often take hold. Enter Microsoft Teams—a single platform designed to simplify collaboration by combining multiple tools in one place. This chapter introduces the concept of Teams, showing how it fits into the broader collaboration landscape, highlighting its key benefits, and giving a glimpse of what you can expect to learn in the chapters ahead.

For years, email has been the go-to method of workplace communication—so much so that many employees live out of their inboxes. Yet email can create problems that modern businesses no longer want to tolerate. Long reply chains, confusing forwarding patterns, and the dreaded "Reply All" can quickly bury critical information. Files get attached, reattached, and lost in a sea of messages, leading to version-control nightmares. And let's not forget how easy it is to accidentally leave someone off an important thread, or to miss an email entirely when your inbox is bursting at the seams.

Adding to these headaches is the fact that email lacks real-time interaction. People send messages, wait hours or days for responses, and often lose momentum on urgent tasks. It's like trying to hold a conversation through postcards: if you're not careful, tasks or decisions can drag out far longer than necessary.

As workplaces adapted to faster, more collaborative environments, a new wave of tools emerged to address email's shortcomings. Slack is well-known for its channel-based messaging, letting teams sort conversations by topic. Zoom skyrocketed in popularity as a straightforward video calling solution, especially in the era of increased remote and hybrid work. These tools showed organizations that real-time messaging, file sharing, and quick video chats could replace unwieldy email chains.

However, having a separate app for chat, another for video calls, and yet another for file storage can feel like juggling three or four different systems. One moment you're messaging a coworker on Slack, the next you're scrambling to open a Zoom link, and later you're searching a random file-sharing service for an attachment. If each platform requires its own login and interface, employees may spend as much time switching between apps as they do working on actual tasks.

Microsoft Teams stands out because it's designed to be an all-in-one collaboration hub. Instead of forcing you to jump between separate apps, Teams integrates chat, video conferencing, file storage, and more into a cohesive package. Teams also feels familiar to anyone who has used Microsoft Word, Excel, or PowerPoint, because it lives under the umbrella of Microsoft 365. That means it benefits from tight integration with Outlook for calendars and email, SharePoint for document management, and OneDrive for personal file storage.

So, while Slack might excel in fast-paced chat and Zoom might shine in large-scale video calls, Teams covers those bases in one environment—plus it hooks directly into the rest of the Microsoft ecosystem that countless organizations already rely on. For many everyday users, this consolidation offers fewer passwords, simpler navigation, and a sense that all your work tools can be accessed from a single screen.

The most obvious perk of Teams is how it bundles communication modes together. You can send a quick message to your colleague in a private chat, schedule a video call with your entire department, or share a file in a channel—without needing to swap apps. For most users, this means fewer browser tabs and fewer "which program was I using for that again?" moments.

Channels within Teams let groups focus on specific projects or topics. Instead of sifting through long email chains, you can drop into a channel and see the entire discussion history at a glance. Files shared in that channel remain in one easy-to-find location, so you never have to search your email for the right version. If you need to escalate a text-based conversation to a face-to-face chat, you can jump straight into a video call without leaving Teams.

In many organizations, employees find themselves forced to learn multiple systems—one for messages, one for project tasks, and another for storing documents. While each service might excel at one thing, the constant switching can chip away at productivity. Teams aims to minimize this problem by seamlessly merging multiple functions under one roof.

This approach is particularly beneficial for those who are less tech-savvy or simply don't have the time to learn multiple platforms. If your entire workday can be anchored in Teams, you're more likely to master its features quickly and less likely to miss urgent pings or notifications. And if your organization already licenses Microsoft 365, the cost of adopting Teams is often covered, meaning no additional platform fees or complications.

Over the next few chapters, you'll explore how Teams structures communication around channels, direct chats, and organized video meetings. You'll learn about the ways in which files are stored and managed, so you can maintain a single source of truth for your documents. You'll also see how Teams handles roles and permissions—important topics if you want to invite external guests or share sensitive information.

We'll go beyond the basics, touching on topics like user adoption strategies (useful if you're encouraging coworkers to embrace Teams), data considerations (like residency and compliance), and how to tailor Teams to fit your daily work processes. Expect chapters dedicated to:

- **Licensing & Setup** – A user-friendly look at how you might be licensed, and what features you can expect.
- **User Roles & Guest Access** – Understanding how you, as an end user, can interact with coworkers or external partners safely.

- **Real-World Usage** – Practical examples of day-to-day communication, ways to reduce email, and success stories from others who have mastered Teams.

Throughout this book, you'll gain insights on reducing email dependency, fostering real-time collaboration, and staying organized. Even if you're comfortable with your current workflow, adopting Teams can free up mental space and time by centralizing your tasks. And as you grow more adept, you might be the person who helps others catch on faster—becoming a Teams champion in your own department or among your friends in the organization.

Remember, Teams is evolving rapidly. By the time you finish reading this, Microsoft may have introduced another new feature or integration. Learning how to adapt quickly will serve you well, not just in Teams but in the modern workplace overall.

Sarah's Story

Sarah had been at 365 Strategies for just a couple of months when she realized her inbox was out of control. She'd come from a smaller organization where a single shared inbox and a handful of direct emails per day sufficed. Now, working in a bustling department, she felt like her morning ritual was deleting junk mail, scanning endless reply-all chains, and sifting through attachments to find the correct file versions.

One afternoon, her colleague Jerome casually mentioned, "Why don't you check the Teams channel for that file?" Sarah shot him a puzzled look—she knew 365 Strategies subscribed to Microsoft 365, but she'd never tried Teams. Jerome opened Teams on his computer and showed her a neatly organized layout of channels dedicated to various projects. He clicked on the relevant channel, scrolled to a conversation thread, and there was the file she'd been looking for, already pinned for easy access.

She was intrigued. The idea of having chat, files, and even video calls in a single window sounded too good to be true, especially given her daily email battles. Then Jerome demonstrated how he could ping their boss with an "@mention" to ask a quick question, and even start a spontaneous video call if they needed immediate clarification. No searching for links, no scheduling a separate meeting—just a seamless transition from text to face-to-face.

A part of Sarah still wondered if this was just another tool she'd have to learn—would she really save time? But seeing how quickly Jerome navigated, she sensed it might be exactly what she needed. The best part was that her manager had been encouraging the department to move away from bloated email chains and adopt a single platform for collaboration. Perhaps this was the nudge Sarah needed.

As she logged into Teams for the first time, she was greeted with a friendly interface that integrated with her Outlook calendar. She immediately spotted a channel labeled "Marketing Campaign Ideas," noticing pinned files and an active conversation about a new client proposal. Scrolling through, she realized she could get up to speed on an entire week's worth of discussions in just a few minutes—something that would have required sifting through who-knows-how-many emails in her inbox.

In that moment, Sarah felt a mix of relief and excitement. If Teams could help her trim her inbox clutter and keep all essential projects in view, it might be a game-changer. Little did she know that this was only the beginning of her Teams journey. She glanced at the tabs labeled "Files," "Posts," and "Meeting," eager to see how each would fit into her daily routine. With a sense of renewed optimism, Sarah decided to explore more of Teams' features, finding hope in a simpler, more organized approach to work.

CHAPTER 2: UNDERSTANDING LICENSING AND GETTING SET UP

When you first open Microsoft Teams, it feels like stepping into a spacious virtual office—complete with chat rooms (called channels), meeting spaces, and file cabinets. But how you experience Teams can depend on your organization's license, as well as which version of the app you're using: desktop, web, or mobile. In this chapter, we'll demystify licensing options and guide you through the simple steps for installing Teams. By the end, you'll know what to expect when you sign in for the first time and how to navigate common pitfalls—so you can start collaborating without stress.

1. Licensing Options

Microsoft offers a free version of Teams for individuals and small groups who want a quick way to chat, share files, and hold video calls without any commitment. This free tier can be sufficient if you're collaborating with a small team or exploring the platform informally. However, the free version has some limitations—like a smaller file storage quota, maximum participant limits in meetings, and fewer administrative controls.

In contrast, most midsize and larger organizations use Microsoft 365 subscriptions—packages that include Outlook email, OneDrive storage, and Office apps such as Word, Excel, and PowerPoint. These subscriptions often come with Teams already included. If your company provides you with a Microsoft 365 work account, there's a good chance you already have access to Teams without needing to pay anything extra. This subscription-based approach typically unlocks more features, such as the ability to schedule webinars, record meetings, and enjoy tighter security measures.

Some organizations use Microsoft's Enterprise license tiers (like E1, E3, or E5). While the details of each tier can get technical, here's what matters to you as a user:

- **E1**: Basic features for online collaboration, including Teams for web-based chat and meetings. You might not have the full desktop Office apps, but you can still access Word, Excel, and PowerPoint online.

- **E3**: A step up that often includes more advanced compliance features, archiving, and the full suite of Office desktop apps. For you, that might mean deeper integration with Outlook, SharePoint, or advanced meeting capabilities.

- **E5**: Typically adds enhanced security and analytics. You might see advanced telephony options in Teams or more sophisticated data protection tools.

The main takeaway is that your exact capabilities—like maximum meeting size, recording options, or advanced collaboration tools—could vary based on which tier your organization has chosen. If you notice that some coworkers can record meetings or use certain features you can't, they might be on a higher license tier (or your admin might have toggled those features off for your group).

2. Setup Nuances: Desktop vs. Web vs. Mobile

- **Desktop App**: Installing Teams on your Windows or Mac computer is usually straightforward. If your company manages your device, the Teams app might already be pre-installed. Otherwise, you can download it from the official Microsoft site. Look for a button that says "Download Teams," run the installer, and follow the prompts. This version typically offers the richest feature set, including more robust settings and offline capabilities (like drafting messages or notes without an internet connection).

- **Web App**: If you prefer not to install anything—or you're working on a shared or locked-down machine—you can use Teams directly in your web browser. Simply navigate to teams.microsoft.com and log in with your Microsoft 365 account. The web version closely resembles the desktop layout but can feel slightly slower or less responsive if you have many channels and chats open. Certain advanced functions, like custom backgrounds in video meetings, may be limited in some browsers.

- **Mobile App**: For on-the-go collaboration, the Teams mobile app is available on iOS and Android. Installing it from your device's app store is simple. Once installed, log in with your Microsoft 365 account, and you'll see your chats and teams synced automatically. This mobile experience is great for quick check-ins, short calls, or scanning notifications, though it's not ideal for heavy document editing or multitasking during lengthy meetings.

Core Differences in Functionality

- **Desktop vs. Web**: The desktop app often runs faster and lets you use certain advanced features (like background blur in meetings or local file sync) that might be hit-or-miss in the browser. The desktop notification system also tends to be more reliable.

- **Web vs. Mobile**: The web version usually mirrors the desktop's major functions, but advanced scheduling or heavy file sharing might be less convenient. Mobile is ideal for quick access—like responding to chat messages or joining a meeting in transit—but can be cumbersome for tasks that require multiple open windows (like simultaneously editing a document while referencing another channel).

- **Desktop vs. Mobile**: If you're co-authoring large files or running multiple conversations at once, the desktop experience usually wins. Mobile excels in short bursts, letting you respond to urgent messages anytime and anywhere.

Ultimately, most employees use a mix of these options. A project manager might rely on the desktop app during the workday, switch to mobile while traveling, and occasionally open the web app on a personal device if they need quick access.

3. Signing In and Navigating First Steps

1. **Open the App or Website**: Double-click the Teams icon on your desktop or navigate to teams.microsoft.com in your browser.

2. **Enter Your Work Credentials**: Use the same email and password you would for Outlook, OneDrive, or other Microsoft 365 apps.

3. **Complete Multi-Factor Authentication (If Required)**: Many organizations require a secondary code via a text message or authenticator app for added security. Follow the on-screen prompts.

4. **Select Your Organization**: If you're part of multiple organizations or have guest access to other tenants, Teams may prompt you to pick which org you want to open first.

5. **Explore the Interface**: Once you're in, you'll see the left-hand navigation bar: Activity, Chat, Teams, Calendar, and Files. Click around to see what's there. Don't be afraid to open a channel or chat to see how discussions are structured.

Common Pitfalls (e.g., Not Seeing Certain Features if You Have a Lighter License)

- **License-Related Missing Features**: If you notice you can't schedule a webinar or record a meeting, it could be that your license tier doesn't include it. You might see a grayed-out button or no option at all. Ask your admin if you think you need that feature.

- **Incorrect Credentials**: Sometimes employees have multiple Microsoft accounts—for instance, one personal and one for work. Make sure you're using your work credentials. Otherwise, you might find yourself in a personal Teams environment instead.

- **Location or Language Settings**: The default language might not match your preference if you're in a global organization. Adjust your profile settings if the date/time format or language isn't what you expect.

- **Notification Overload**: The default notifications might feel overwhelming at first. We'll delve deeper into customizing notifications later, but be aware you can toggle or tune them under Settings > Notifications.

As you explore the interface, keep an eye on the "Help" icon (usually near the bottom left). Microsoft frequently updates its in-app help resources, which can be a lifesaver if you have a quick question about a button or setting.

Sarah's Story

When Sarah realized she already had a Microsoft 365 account that included Teams, she felt a surge of relief—no need to purchase anything or wrestle with complicated install steps. At first, she tried out the web version at her desk. Within seconds of typing in her 365 Strategies email and password, she was greeted by a neat interface showing several channels, each labeled with the name of a project or department.

Curious to see if the desktop app offered more features, Sarah downloaded it from the official Microsoft site. The installer finished in minutes, and when she launched the app, she was happy to see the same channels she'd viewed online appeared automatically. "At least I won't have to rebuild everything," she thought. In exploring the desktop UI, she noticed a few cool extras—like the option to pin important chats for quick access and a notifications panel that integrated smoothly with her system tray.

Next, Sarah grabbed her phone and installed the Teams mobile app. She initially worried the small screen might be too cramped for real work, but after logging in, she found it easy to respond to chat messages and scan the recent Activity feed. A coworker pinged her about a client meeting, and with just a tap, she joined a quick audio call to confirm some details. Sarah was impressed—no more fumbling for a Zoom link or emailing back and forth to schedule a last-minute discussion.

The only snag she hit was attempting to record a meeting. The "Start Recording" button didn't appear for her, which led to some confusion until she mentioned it to a colleague. That colleague explained that her Microsoft 365 Business Basic license at 365 Strategies didn't come with advanced meeting recordings. They assured her that if she needed to record something critical, she could invite one of the senior leads with a higher-tier license to handle it. This was a valuable lesson: even though Teams seemed universal, certain extra capabilities hinged on specific licensing arrangements.

Over the next few days, Sarah became comfortable switching between desktop, web, and mobile versions of Teams. Each morning, she opened the desktop app to review any overnight channel updates. In the afternoon, if she left the office for a client meeting, she'd keep an eye on notifications via her phone. And during a quick break, she might hop on the web version from a colleague's computer, logging into her account without needing to install anything.

As she settled into this routine, she realized how stress-free it felt. No more rummaging through email to find which attachments were up to date, no more missing messages if she stepped away from her desk. Sure, she'd have to learn some of Teams' finer points, like setting up channels properly or managing notifications, but the initial jump was smoother than she'd expected. And the best part? She already had everything she needed thanks to her existing Microsoft 365 license.

By the end of the week, Sarah couldn't imagine going back to an environment where every function—email, chat, file sharing—lived on a different app. Although she knew there was still more to master, these first steps had already convinced her that Teams was a worthy cornerstone for daily collaboration at 365 Strategies.

CHAPTER 3: USER ROLES VS. GUEST ACCESS—WHAT YOU NEED TO KNOW

As you step more fully into using Microsoft Teams, you'll notice that not everyone in a Team has the same level of control. Some people can add new channels or even remove members, while others can simply post messages and upload files. You might also discover there's a role called "Guest," which is designed for external collaborators like freelance designers or vendors. This chapter explores the different user roles in Microsoft Teams—Owners, Members, and Guests—and illustrates how these distinctions influence day-to-day teamwork. We'll also look at the implications of inviting external people into your workspace, including a few best practices for keeping your organization's data secure.

Microsoft Teams defines three primary roles within a team: Owners, Members, and Guests. Although these might sound like IT-oriented terms, each has a direct impact on your daily collaboration activities.

- **Owners**: Think of Owners as the people who created or oversee the team. They have the most control over team settings. An Owner can add or remove members, change channels' privacy, alter the team's name, and adjust permissions for who can post or delete messages. Typically, there are one or two Owners per team—often the project lead, department manager, or someone in a supervisory role. From a user's standpoint, if you ever need a new channel created or want to tweak how the team is structured, it's the Owner you'll ask.

- **Members**: Most employees in a team will be Members. Members can post messages, upload files, create or participate in channels, and schedule meetings—basically, everything needed to do their daily tasks. However, they cannot drastically modify the team's structure (for example, they can't delete the entire team or override certain privacy settings). This balance ensures that day-to-day collaboration flows smoothly without giving everyone the ability to make major changes that could disrupt others.

- **Guests**: Guests are external collaborators who aren't part of your organization's Microsoft 365 tenant. You might invite them to a channel or team space if they're working on a project alongside your internal staff. Guests are typically restricted in what they can see and do compared to full Members. For instance, a Guest might be allowed to view and upload files in a designated channel but not have the rights to rename channels or access other sensitive parts of your Teams environment. The main reason for these limitations is security—your company wants to be sure external folks only see relevant information and don't accidentally stumble upon confidential data.

Within each team, you'll see various channels—some are open to all Members, while others might be private. Owners generally decide which channels exist and who can access private channels. Members can contribute to any channels they're part of, posting updates, commenting on others' posts, and uploading documents. Guests can do the same in the channels they're invited to but might be locked out of certain capabilities, like creating new private channels or viewing the entire team's membership directory.

From the perspective of an everyday user, it's helpful to know if you're an Owner or a Member in the teams you participate in. If you're an Owner, you'll see additional settings under the team's management options—like "Manage Team." If you're a Member, you'll still have the freedom to collaborate extensively but may need to request help from an Owner if you want structural or permission changes.

Guest access can be incredibly convenient when you're working with people outside your company. For example:

- **Freelance Designers**: If you're collaborating on marketing campaigns, you might want the designer to see ongoing ideas, quickly comment on visuals, or upload updated graphics without emailing large files back and forth.

- **Consultants**: A consultant offering expertise on process improvements can review discussions in relevant channels, respond to queries in real time, and share quick tips or documents directly in your workspace.

- **Vendors**: If you rely on a particular supplier or vendor, bringing them into a channel where they can see your requests and timelines can reduce miscommunication.

By granting them Guest status instead of a full Member role, you ensure they only see the channels and files that pertain to their tasks, maintaining privacy for other internal projects.

Basic Do's and Don'ts

- **Do** confirm with an Owner or your manager that it's appropriate to add a specific Guest. Some organizations require approval before letting external users into their environment.

- **Do** add Guests to only the channels they truly need. Restricting them to a single project channel can reduce confusion and the risk of oversharing.

- **Do** set clear expectations. Let your external collaborator know how to navigate Teams, which channel they should post in, and who to tag for quick answers.

- **Don't** share sensitive or confidential documents without verifying that it's within policy.

- **Don't** give Guests Owner privileges. That would allow them to alter fundamental team settings, which generally isn't advisable unless there's a compelling reason.

Once a Guest is added, they'll typically receive an email invitation prompting them to join your team or channel. If your organization uses multi-factor authentication or other security measures, they may need to follow those steps as well. It's a good idea to send them a quick orientation message explaining how to post in the channel or where to find files—especially if they're new to Microsoft Teams.

As soon as a Guest is part of your team, they can potentially view and download files shared in the channels they have access to. Keep in mind:

- **Label Documents Clearly**: If a file is sensitive or for internal eyes only, double-check the channel or folder location before uploading.

- **Use Private Channels for Confidential Work**: If your team deals with highly sensitive information, you might create a private channel specifically for internal staff, shielding it from external guests. An Owner can help set this up.

- **Understand Version History**: If a Guest edits a file shared in a channel, that change is visible in the file's version history. This helps keep track of who did what but also means you can revert if needed.

Sometimes, you might feel restricted in your ability to add or manage guests, or you may need to adjust channel privacy settings. That's when you'd consult either:

1. **Your Team Owner**: They might grant you or your department more leeway in managing guest access.

2. **IT or a Microsoft 365 Admin**: If your company has a strict security policy, IT might need to handle external invitations or special permissions. For instance, regulated industries often have extra layers of scrutiny before letting external users into any part of the system.

If you're unsure whether you can share a particular document with an external collaborator, it's better to ask your IT or manager than to risk a potential data breach.

Sarah's Story

A few weeks into using Microsoft Teams, Sarah found herself on a new marketing project that required specialized input from an external consultant. The consultant, Danielle, had a background in consumer behavior and was slated to help 365 Strategies refine its brand messaging.

Sarah initially thought she'd just email Danielle slides and keep track of her comments in separate documents. But then she remembered how chatty and visually oriented her colleagues were when working in Teams channels. Would it be easier if Danielle could see the entire conversation about upcoming campaigns, rather than relying on patchwork updates? Sarah decided to explore the idea of adding Danielle as a guest.

To do this, she went to the "Brand Refresh Project" team in Teams, where she found the option to add a new member. She typed in Danielle's email address and noticed a pop-up informing her that this address was outside 365 Strategies' domain. The system automatically flagged it as a Guest invitation. Recalling that certain channels contained confidential budget data, Sarah double-checked with her manager and discovered they'd created a separate, open channel specifically for external collaborators. Her manager assured her that the finance-related channels were locked down to internal staff only.

Sarah clicked "Add," and Danielle received an email invitation to join the "Brand Refresh Collab" channel. The next morning, Danielle posted a greeting in the channel's chat and attached a creative brief. Sarah was thrilled. Finally, a single location where everyone on the marketing team, plus Danielle, could discuss ideas without scattering documents across countless emails.

As they moved forward, Sarah noticed subtle differences in Danielle's experience as a Guest. Danielle couldn't create private channels on her own, nor could she tweak certain team settings. This was fine, as Danielle only needed to share files and comment on existing threads. However, the arrangement also highlighted the importance of limiting who saw what. One day, Danielle mentioned she couldn't see a particular budget spreadsheet that Sarah assumed she could access. Realizing that document lived in a more confidential channel, Sarah quickly rectified the confusion by confirming the file's location and clarifying that they wouldn't open that data to external partners.

The process gave Sarah a deeper understanding of how roles and permissions worked. She realized it wasn't just an IT concept—it directly affected day-to-day collaboration. Because Danielle was labeled as a Guest, she could only see relevant channels, which prevented accidental exposure of sensitive corporate information. Sarah also felt reassured that any potential security risks were minimized.

The next hurdle came when Sarah wanted Danielle's input on a draft press release stored in another channel. Sarah found she couldn't simply share the link with Danielle because that channel remained internal-only. Instead, she invited her manager to weigh in on whether to open that channel or move the document to the "Brand Refresh Collab" space. In the end, they decided to move the press release to a folder accessible to both internal members and Danielle. This small extra step reminded Sarah how crucial it was to track file locations in Teams.

Within just a week of working together, Sarah saw how much time they saved by letting Danielle jump into discussions, share her expertise in real time, and revise creative assets directly in Teams. No lengthy email threads, no accidental "reply-all" fiascos, and no mixed-up file versions. Sure, Sarah had to remain cautious about what data Danielle could see, but the payoff was clear: external collaboration thrived when structured around well-defined roles and channels.

By the project's conclusion, Sarah felt far more confident about managing guest access. She knew exactly why limiting guests to specific channels was beneficial, how to communicate with her manager or an Owner if she needed advanced permissions, and which channels absolutely had to stay internal. This blend of convenience and security reassured Sarah that Teams could handle both day-to-day internal chatter and more formal partnerships with external professionals.

Returning to her desk at the end of the day, Sarah reflected on how far she'd come since first downloading Teams. Learning about roles, permissions, and guest access wasn't just about pushing the right buttons; it was about empowering the right people—colleagues and external collaborators—to contribute effectively, all while safeguarding what needed to remain confidential. For Sarah, it was another step in discovering how Teams could streamline her work life at 365 Strategies.

CHAPTER 4: DATA RESIDENCY AND COMPLIANCE

Modern organizations often manage a staggering amount of information—everything from customer data to internal reports on future products. As an everyday user of Microsoft Teams, you might occasionally wonder why your company seems so strict about where files are stored or how certain documents are shared. In this chapter, we'll clarify some key reasons behind these rules. We'll look at data residency (the concept of where your data physically resides), explore simple security steps you can take on both desktop and mobile, and highlight scenarios where you should think twice before uploading a file. By understanding these principles, you'll be better prepared to keep sensitive information safe and stay on the right side of corporate policies and legal requirements.

"Data residency" refers to the physical location or geographical region where your company's data is stored or processed. In the past, businesses often kept all their servers in an on-site data center. Today, with cloud-based solutions like Microsoft 365, data might be housed in data centers across different regions—sometimes even different countries.

From a user's perspective, you might notice data residency concerns when your company gives specific guidelines on storing files in certain Teams channels or SharePoint sites. For instance, if you're in the EU, your organization could insist that all EU-related data stays within EU-based data centers to meet local regulations. Similarly, a U.S. healthcare provider might use specialized channels for patient information to maintain HIPAA compliance. While these nuances can feel invisible in day-to-day use, they shape how you share files, send messages, or allow guest access to your channels.

Many regions impose regulations that govern how personal or confidential data is handled. Two well-known examples are:

- **GDPR (General Data Protection Regulation)**: This European Union regulation mandates strict guidelines for processing and storing personal data of EU residents. Even if your office isn't in Europe, you could be subject to GDPR if you handle EU citizen data.

- **HIPAA (Health Insurance Portability and Accountability Act)**: In the United States, HIPAA protects patient health information. Healthcare organizations must follow stringent protocols for how they store or share patient records.

These regulations often influence the features and security settings in Microsoft Teams. For example, organizations might enable certain retention policies to automatically delete old data or restrict file-sharing outside the company. While you might not be directly configuring these policies, understanding they exist can explain why your workplace has rules about which channel you can put sensitive files in or how long chat messages are retained.

Even though Teams makes file-sharing as easy as dragging and dropping a document, it's critical to know when and where you should upload something. Some guidelines might include:

- **Identify Sensitive vs. Non-Sensitive Data**: If you're about to share an internal financial report, a contract with personal info, or a customer list, check your company's policies. There may be a specific channel or library designed to handle this level of confidentiality.

- **Marking Files Clearly**: Some workplaces use labels or tags (e.g., "Confidential," "Internal Only," "Public") to categorize content. Respect these labels when saving or sharing documents. If you're unsure, err on the side of caution and ask.

- **Use Secure Channels**: Your Microsoft Teams environment might have private channels or dedicated "secure" workspaces.

These channels limit who can see and edit the files, which helps keep sensitive information under wraps.

General channels are great for everyday chatter, project updates, or harmless office banter. However, uploading business-critical documents or personally identifiable information (PII) into a general channel might violate internal or external policies. If your organization has set up a "Finance Confidential" channel or an "HR-Restricted" channel, that's your cue to store sensitive files there rather than in a more public location.

Even if your chat is private or you've messaged someone directly, attachments may still be saved somewhere in the Microsoft 365 cloud. That means the same rules apply: if it's sensitive, confirm you're placing it in an approved folder or channel.

Many employees switch between the Teams desktop app at work and the Teams mobile app on their phone or tablet. While this flexibility is convenient, it also introduces more risk if you're not careful:

- **Lock Your Device**: Always enable PIN codes, biometrics, or password locks for your phone. This helps prevent unauthorized access if your phone is lost or stolen.

- **Avoid Public Wi-Fi for Sensitive Tasks**: If you're traveling, be cautious about uploading or viewing confidential documents on open networks, like in cafes or airports. A mobile hotspot or VPN might be safer.

- **Sign Out if Needed**: If you're using a shared device—even a family tablet—remember to sign out of your Teams account to prevent accidental exposure of your work channels.

If your role involves frequent travel, make sure you understand your organization's policy on accessing data from other countries. While traveling, certain compliance regulations (like GDPR) still apply. Also, different regions may have varying privacy laws. Keeping your laptop or mobile app updated with the latest security patches and using approved VPNs or secure access protocols can prevent data leaks.

Sarah's Story

As Sarah grew more confident with Teams, she discovered new ways to collaborate with her colleagues. One day, she needed to share an important client presentation that included sensitive business data—like customer purchase histories and upcoming product pricing. She knew she couldn't just plop it into a general channel, because that might expose details to team members who didn't need access.

Unsure of the exact protocol, Sarah emailed her manager for clarification. He directed her to the company's internal guidelines, which spelled out a simple rule: client data was subject to certain privacy requirements akin to GDPR standards. To ensure compliance, the company had created a "Client Confidential" channel that only approved employees could access. It lived under the marketing team's broader environment, but had tighter settings.

Following the guidelines, Sarah uploaded her presentation to the "Client Confidential" channel. She then pasted a short message in the channel chat, tagging her manager and a few key stakeholders who needed to review the slides. Within minutes, she received feedback right in the channel. She found it far simpler than juggling multiple email attachments—and she felt secure knowing that only those with the correct permissions could see the data.

Her next challenge came when she attended a conference in another city. She wanted to polish some slides and share last-minute updates with her boss. Logging into Teams on her phone, she was about to upload a revised file via hotel Wi-Fi. That's when she recalled the training about public networks and compliance risks. Instead, she tethered to her phone's data connection, ensuring a secure path for transferring files. The extra step took only a moment, and it gave her peace of mind that she wasn't inadvertently exposing confidential client information.

Sarah's diligence paid off. When she returned to 365 Strategies the following week, her manager complimented her on following the correct data handling procedures. He explained that many employees don't realize how crucial it is to store sensitive files in the right channels or use a secure connection when traveling. If Sarah had uploaded the presentation to the wrong spot or used an unprotected public Wi-Fi, the company could have faced compliance risks or a potential data breach.

Over time, Sarah grew more attuned to the lines between "general" project files and data that carried heavier legal or ethical obligations. She also passed along what she learned to a new coworker, emphasizing that yes, Teams was a powerful tool for sharing—but only if you paid attention to which channels were best suited for which documents. This user-level awareness of data residency, security, and compliance might not feel flashy, but it kept her company safe and ensured that Teams remained a trusted workspace for all sorts of collaborative efforts.

CHAPTER 5: WORKING IN TEAMS DAY-TO-DAY—ADOPTION BASICS

The real power of Microsoft Teams becomes clear when you use it in place of traditional channels like email and outdated file-sharing services. Relying on Teams for your day-to-day communication can dramatically simplify how you collaborate with your coworkers, create clarity around tasks, and reduce the constant back-and-forth many of us face. This chapter explores the practical steps you can take to shift from email overload to more efficient conversations, offers a quick look at the core areas of Teams (channels, chats, and meetings), and highlights a few strategies that will help you get comfortable as an everyday Teams user.

For many of us, email has long been a default method for everything from tiny updates to large project distributions. But as Teams becomes your central hub, you might start thinking differently about when and why you hit "Send" on a new email. Instead of forwarding a document to three people and waiting for separate replies, you can drop that file into a Teams channel and engage in real-time discussions. You might also see less redundancy, since adding a file or link directly within a channel means everyone knows where to find the latest version.

Shifting away from email doesn't necessarily mean eliminating it. There will always be occasions where a formal, single-recipient message is appropriate, especially for inter-organizational communications or official memos. However, daily, ongoing conversations often flow more naturally when posted in a channel or via a short chat in Teams. This approach helps keep the entire group informed in one shared space, reducing the chance that someone gets left off an email thread.

If you're unsure which route to take, you can weigh urgency and audience. A quick question about a project status might be ideal for a Teams chat, ensuring you receive a prompt response. If you're broadcasting a company-wide policy update, email might still be the better vehicle. Over time, you'll develop an intuition for the types of communication that thrive in each format.

The three primary ways people collaborate in Teams are channels, chats, and meetings. Channels are essentially topic- or project-oriented spaces where relevant conversations and files can live. Instead of going back to your inbox to find the right email string, you can just open the channel in Teams and view the entire history in one neat feed. Chats are more direct and personal, functioning like instant messaging. They're perfect for quick clarifications or smaller group discussions. Meanwhile, meetings inside Teams offer a fluid way to escalate from text to a live voice or video call, all without leaving the platform.

Bringing these together means you can store important files in channels, coordinate schedules using the Meetings tab, and ask offhand questions in a chat thread—rather than juggling multiple services. Everything becomes accessible from one central dashboard. This integrated approach helps keep your daily routine straightforward. You log in, open Teams, and find what you need: conversations, documents, and scheduled meetings all in one place.

For many people, the biggest initial challenge in Teams is knowing how to stay organized and avoid notification overload. One useful approach is to pin your most frequently used channels, giving you quick access to the projects or departments you work with the most. If you find yourself scrolling every time you open Teams, pinning (or favoriting) a few essential channels can save you time and energy.

Managing notifications is another crucial step in building a sustainable workflow. If you leave all alerts at their defaults, you might receive constant pings for every post in every channel. Some people appreciate that level of visibility, but others prefer a leaner experience. Tailoring notifications means deciding which events trigger a banner or an email, and which ones simply appear in your activity feed. You could choose to only see an alert when you're mentioned directly, or when a channel you follow has an important update, rather than for every comment that rolls in.

The search feature, located at the top of the Teams window, can also be a powerful ally as you settle into using the platform. When you need to track down a conversation or file, typing a keyword in the search bar can jump you to the relevant thread in seconds. This becomes especially handy as your organization's Teams environment grows, preventing you from wading through multiple channels to find one snippet of information.

For users who move around during the day or occasionally work outside the office, the mobile app can be a lifesaver. Installing Teams on your phone or tablet ensures that you don't miss an important chat or meeting invitation when you're away from your desk. Some people even find it quicker to send updates or reply to short questions from the mobile app, sparing them from booting up a laptop for minor tasks.

Overall, adjusting to Teams as a core part of your daily workflow is a matter of experimenting with these features and finding the balance that feels comfortable for you. If you feel overwhelmed, dialing back notifications might help. If you're searching for messages repeatedly, using the search bar or pinned channels could save you time. And if you're constantly emailing documents to the same group of people, dropping those files in a channel may be your next big time-saver.

Sarah's Story

After dipping her toes in the water with her weekly project updates channel, Sarah decided to broaden her Teams usage. She made a conscious effort to send fewer group emails, especially those that involved quick back-and-forth discussion. Whenever she prepared to type a new email, she paused to ask, "Could this conversation fit better as a post in a channel?" Nine times out of ten, the answer was yes.

Initially, a few of her colleagues kept replying via email or forgetting the channel existed. Sarah understood it would take time for everyone to adapt. She continued posting relevant updates in Teams, mentioning team members by name so they'd receive a direct alert. Gradually, people realized the ease of referencing files right next to the conversation about those files, rather than opening multiple windows or forwarding lengthy email chains.

One moment crystallized her appreciation for Teams. She needed real-time feedback on a design layout from three coworkers. Instead of scheduling a formal call, she started a new message in the design channel, tagged each person, and attached the draft. Within minutes, they hopped into the thread, offering suggestions. When two of them started to disagree on layout details, Sarah initiated a short "Meet Now" call directly from that channel, inviting them to join. The three talked it out quickly, updated the draft, and shared the final version back in the same space—no separate scheduling tool, no lost attachments, no extra steps.

While Sarah was thrilled at how seamlessly everything came together, she also learned the importance of managing her own notifications. After receiving alerts for every mention and comment, she realized she needed to tweak her settings so she wouldn't be interrupted whenever someone posted a routine status. A quick visit to the notification settings in Teams allowed her to reduce the less critical pop-ups, limiting them to direct mentions and replies to her posts. This shift helped her maintain focus during heads-down work while still staying looped in on the discussions that needed her input.

Within a couple of months, Sarah felt more in control of her workflow than ever before. She no longer dreaded opening her email in the morning, because many of those back-and-forth chains had migrated into channel conversations where she could skim updates at a glance. Meetings also felt more purposeful; instead of spending large chunks of time sharing information that could have been posted in Teams, discussions zeroed in on bigger decisions.

Looking back on this process, Sarah realized Teams didn't just solve problems—it changed how she approached daily tasks. By centralizing communication and files, she reclaimed hours that had previously been lost to email management. Best of all, she felt a growing confidence that she, and the rest of 365 Strategies, were finally harnessing a tool designed to make teamwork simpler, rather than juggling multiple platforms that never quite fit together.

CHAPTER 6: ONBOARDING CHECKLISTS AND ROLLOUT STRATEGIES

A robust onboarding experience can profoundly shape how new employees perceive Microsoft Teams and integrate it into their workflow. While IT teams and department heads often plan the official rollout, individual users also play a crucial role in guiding newcomers. You might find yourself showing a new coworker which channels to join or walking them through a quick tutorial on how to schedule a meeting. This chapter explores practical steps any user can take to support a smooth onboarding process, sheds light on common rollout strategies (like "big bang" vs. phased approaches), and provides tips for creating a personal onboarding plan that keeps your own use of Teams fresh and adaptable. By recognizing that everyone in an organization has a stake in the successful adoption of Teams, you can help foster a more collaborative culture one new hire at a time.

When a new employee joins your organization, they're juggling countless pieces of information—from understanding company policies to learning people's names and roles. Figuring out how to use Microsoft Teams effectively can be both exciting and overwhelming. For the new hire, having a clear checklist of how to get started is invaluable. If you've been using Teams for a while, you can become an informal mentor, pointing them toward the essentials that you wish you'd known on day one.

A well-organized checklist might include simple tasks such as installing the Teams desktop app, logging in with corporate credentials, and ensuring multi-factor authentication is set up if required by company policy. Once they're in, guiding them to the primary channels relevant to their role helps them build context. For instance, if they're joining a marketing team, direct them to the "Campaign Ideas" channel or any private channels where sensitive material is discussed. By channeling them to the right spaces immediately, you spare them the confusion of scrolling through an entire list of channels to figure out which ones apply to their projects.

Even if Human Resources or IT provides some general orientation on Teams, you (as a colleague) likely have firsthand tips about daily usage that no official guide can fully capture. Let them know if your department uses specific naming conventions for files or if there's a set of pinned channels they should keep an eye on. You might also point out small nuances—maybe your team uses "General" channels for broad announcements but expects quick questions to be posted in more focused project channels. This friendly, peer-driven approach can go a long way in making new hires feel supported as they dip their toes into Teams for the first time.

Another aspect of structured onboarding is clarifying responsibilities. While HR might ensure the new hire's account is created and licensed appropriately, individuals often have to set up their notification preferences, join additional teams if needed, and practice scheduling a meeting or uploading a file. Encouraging them to perform these tasks early—and reassuring them that it's okay to make mistakes—helps them get comfortable. Rather than passively absorbing a slideshow on Teams, they're actively exploring its features from day one.

Organizations typically adopt one of two broad strategies when introducing Microsoft Teams. The "big bang" approach means everyone in the company is given access around the same time, with a clear directive to move most communications into Teams. This approach can be exhilarating—suddenly, you find that nearly every colleague is available via a Team chat or channel. But it can also be chaotic, particularly if some employees resist change or if the rollout lacks proper training resources. As a user, you might notice an initial flood of new channels and messages as people try to find their footing.

On the other end of the spectrum, the phased rollout starts small. An organization might select one or two departments that volunteer to adopt Teams first. These early adopters experiment, uncover potential pitfalls, and refine best practices before the tool expands to other areas. By the time more teams join, some lessons have been learned, and guidelines are clearer. For instance, you might see standardized naming for channels, or specific instructions on how to handle external guests. As a user who's already in the pilot group, you become an informal ambassador—ready to explain how your team overcame early hiccups.

From a day-to-day standpoint, adapting to a "big bang" means you'll likely see a rapid increase in channels, chats, and meeting invites in Teams. If your organization invests in training, pay attention to any workshops or Q&A sessions so that you can master features quickly. If training resources are minimal, you may need to rely on colleagues, internal guides, or your own exploration to keep up. In a phased rollout, you might experience a slower build-up of activity, allowing you time to gradually move away from old habits (like emailing large attachments) and adopt more of Teams' features without feeling swamped.

As a user, it helps to appreciate which approach your organization has chosen. If it's a big bang, brace yourself for a whirlwind. If it's phased, recognize that your department might not have full Teams functionality until the later stages. In both scenarios, keep in mind that every coworker handles change differently. Some will happily jump into video chats and pinned channels, while others will cling to email out of habit. Offering empathy and a bit of gentle guidance can create a smoother transition, no matter the rollout strategy.

Even if you're not new to the company, you might be new to Teams—or you might feel like you never really learned it beyond basic chat functions. Crafting your own mini "onboarding plan" can help you stay curious and leverage the platform more fully.

For starters, consider your notification settings. Many users complain about getting too many pop-up alerts, which can lead to ignoring them altogether. Spending time in Settings to decide which channels deserve real-time notifications and which can be silently updated in your activity feed is key to avoiding alert fatigue. You might also explore how to set

"Quiet Hours" in the mobile app, so you don't receive work-related buzzes late at night.

Next, try exploring a new feature each week. Perhaps one week, you focus on the search bar to learn how to locate older messages or files more quickly. Another week, you might experiment with scheduling a short meeting and sharing your screen to walk a coworker through a new proposal. This incremental approach is less daunting than trying to master every aspect of Teams in a single day.

Practicing with test calls or "dummy" channels can also accelerate your comfort level. If you're uncertain about how to share a file or enable background blur in a video call, invite a willing colleague (or even your own personal account if your organization allows it) and run a small test. The difference between reading about a feature and actually clicking the buttons yourself is huge. Once you've succeeded in a low-stakes environment, you'll feel more confident when you need to apply these skills to real project channels and important meetings.

Finally, don't underestimate the value of existing training resources. Microsoft offers a variety of quick start guides and tutorial videos. Some organizations develop their own knowledge base with step-by-step instructions tailored to internal processes. If you're pressed for time, even scanning a short "Teams Tips" article once a week can help you pick up new shortcuts, such as how to reply quickly to a channel post or how to tag a specific group of people with an @mention. Over time, these small discoveries add up, making Teams feel second nature rather than another app you have to fight with daily.

Sarah's Story

When Sarah learned that a new coworker, Tia, had joined 365 Strategies, she decided to reach out and offer some guidance on Microsoft Teams. She remembered her own initial confusion—a swirl of channels, uncertain mention of "Owners" and "Members," and a haze of notifications that seemed to pop up every time someone breathed in the next channel over. Determined to make Tia's experience smoother, Sarah drew on her own notes and formed a simple checklist.

On Tia's first morning, Sarah set aside a few minutes to walk her through installing the Teams desktop app and signing in with her corporate account. Once Tia was in, Sarah showed her how to pin the department's three main channels. Tia seemed relieved to know she didn't have to scroll endlessly, hunting for the right place to post. Sarah also demonstrated how to navigate the "General" channel for broad announcements versus specific project channels for more focused discussions.

After Tia felt comfortable with the basics, Sarah introduced her to scheduling a brief "test meeting" in Teams. They hopped on a short call right then and there, exploring how to share a presentation slide and chatting about Tia's previous job. Although Tia was shy about appearing on video, she appreciated the clarity of seeing how a meeting invite worked and how easy it was to switch from typing in chat to speaking directly.

Later that week, Tia confided that she found the default notifications overwhelming, especially when certain coworkers posted multiple messages back-to-back. Sarah suggested customizing channel notifications, explaining that Tia could choose to only receive alerts when she was @mentioned directly. Intrigued, Tia spent a bit of time in her notification settings, emerging with a more streamlined experience. She thanked Sarah for the tip, adding that she'd already started to enjoy how integrated everything felt. Instead of juggling multiple apps for chat, file sharing, and scheduling calls, she could stay within Teams for most of her needs.

At the same time, Sarah noticed that 365 Strategies was gearing up for a "big bang" approach in another region of the company. While Sarah's department had adopted Teams in phases, a sister department overseas was about to come online in one massive rollout. Sarah wondered how that group would handle the deluge of new channels and the inevitable early confusion. She silently congratulated herself on being part of a slower adoption phase, where she and her colleagues had time to shape the best channel structures and refine naming conventions.

Before the end of Tia's first month, Sarah checked in again. Tia had started following a personal onboarding plan of her own. Each week, she practiced one new Teams trick. In week one, she learned to organize pinned chats, so she could quickly reference direct messages from her manager. In week two, she discovered advanced search filters, which helped her retrieve a conversation from two weeks prior without scrolling endlessly. And in week three, she played around with meeting recordings, noticing that she needed to be aware of certain licensing issues if she wanted to save recordings for later review.

Looking back on the entire process, Sarah realized how much influence individual users have over a new hire's success with Teams. Even though Tia had some orientation materials from HR, the real breakthrough moments came from personal guidance—like test calls, pinned channels, and the nitty-gritty of managing notifications. Sarah found the experience rewarding, not only because she was helping Tia acclimate but also because she sharpened her own Teams knowledge by teaching someone else.

By embracing these onboarding strategies—whether official or informal—Sarah saw how an organization's adoption of Teams could flourish. Newcomers felt more confident, existing employees fine-tuned their skills, and the entire department benefited from a smoother, more consistent way of communicating. Over time, she hoped that the entire company would share a common baseline of Teams proficiency, leaving behind scattered email chains and disjointed project management tactics once and for all. And if that required a few more checklists and friendly one-on-one sessions, Sarah was happy to oblige. After all, she knew firsthand how big a difference it made to have someone patiently show you the ropes in a platform as versatile as Microsoft Teams.

CHAPTER 7: BEST PRACTICES FOR TEAMWIDE ENGAGEMENT

Implementing Microsoft Teams within a single department can bring noticeable benefits—reduced email threads, quicker collaboration on projects, and a more transparent view of tasks in progress. However, those wins are often amplified when multiple departments or even the entire organization embraces Teams together. Achieving this broader adoption isn't just about an official rollout plan; it also hinges on everyday users championing the platform and guiding their colleagues toward its simpler, more organized approach to work. In this chapter, we'll look at how you can encourage those around you to use Teams more effectively, show ways to support hesitant coworkers, and explore how to measure personal wins that validate why Teams is worth the switch.

Many people are hesitant to change their communication habits, especially if they've relied on email for years or are reluctant to learn a new tool. Sometimes, small gestures from fellow employees can be the tipping point that helps them realize how Teams might solve persistent frustrations. One straightforward way to nudge people is by tagging them directly in a channel. If you're having a conversation about a shared project, mentioning a colleague with "@Name" ensures they see the thread. It also subtly invites them to answer within Teams instead of sending a reply via email.

Uploading relevant files to the channel rather than attaching them to emails can also entice your coworkers to visit Teams more frequently. Instead of forwarding the same deck to five people, post it in the channel where you've been discussing the project. That single act can demonstrate how easily everyone can comment, reference past versions, and collectively keep track of changes. When your teammates realize they no longer have to sift through old email chains to find the right attachment, they often warm up to Teams quickly.

You can also spark engagement by encouraging interactive elements that aren't as seamless over email. For instance, quick polls or simple surveys posted in a channel allow the entire team to respond at once, with results visible in real time. This immediate feedback is not only more fun but more efficient. Instead of sorting out separate email replies, you have a consolidated poll and an instant snapshot of everyone's preferences or availability. When people see how easily these features streamline decision-making, they may become more receptive to using Teams for other daily tasks.

Another tactic is highlighting the practical advantages of real-time communication. If your team typically debates an issue over a series of emails spanning multiple days, you might propose jumping on a quick channel conversation or a short, ad-hoc meeting in Teams. Seeing how swiftly a resolution comes about—sometimes in a matter of minutes— can drive home the point that Teams reduces the friction inherent in slower, more cumbersome methods.

Finally, it helps to celebrate small wins along the way. Any time you notice a direct benefit of using Teams—fewer lost attachments, quicker decisions, or one conversation thread that replaced dozens of emails— mention it during a department meeting or in the general channel. By calling attention to these improvements, you reinforce why adopting Teams is worth the learning curve. Positive reinforcement can do wonders in shifting a colleague's perspective from "another tool I have to learn" to "a platform that actually makes my work easier."

Even the best official training programs can't anticipate every question or scenario that surfaces. That's why informal "buddy" or champion systems often play a critical role in sustained Teams adoption. If you feel comfortable navigating Teams—perhaps you've experimented with scheduling video calls, customizing channels, or integrating apps like Planner—you can position yourself as a friendly point of reference for coworkers who need help. These champion-like figures reduce the intimidation factor. Sometimes, people are more likely to ask a peer for help than to submit a formal request to IT or wade through detailed tutorials.

Over time, you might notice certain colleagues remain skeptical or see Teams as an unnecessary complication. Rather than confront them aggressively, try a more empathetic approach. Show them real examples of how you saved time or avoided confusion by keeping a project's discussions in a single channel. Sometimes a short demonstration—a side-by-side view of a channel conversation plus the relevant files—can illustrate how Teams unifies tasks that might otherwise live in separate apps. This tangible proof often resonates more than any abstract explanation.

Another way to offer support is by acknowledging that the shift can be disorienting, especially for those who have established routines around email folders or older communication tools. You might suggest a gradual adoption approach, such as encouraging them to post quick questions in Teams while still relying on email for formal messages. Over time, as they see the convenience of immediate responses or pinned documents, they may expand their usage. If they do, celebrating that small progress can help them feel validated and motivated to keep exploring Teams' features.

Supporting each other also means sharing success stories within your own department or organization. If a small group of employees overcame an old pain point—like version-control chaos on spreadsheets—by pivoting those documents into Teams, encourage them to talk about how that's been working. Hearing a personal testimonial from someone who faced the same struggles can be more persuasive than a general tutorial or top-down directive. This grassroots, peer-driven method often strengthens adoption more effectively than any single memo or training session could.

You don't need advanced analytics or formal metrics to realize the impact of using Teams day-to-day. Even so, paying attention to certain indicators can help you quantify (and celebrate) your progress. For example, some employees keep a rough tally of how many emails they send per week—especially group emails intended for project updates. If you see that number gradually decreasing while your channel activity rises, it suggests you're consolidating communication in a more open, transparent place.

Time saved is another intangible but real gain. If you notice that retrieving an important conversation used to involve digging through your inbox for five minutes, and now you locate the thread in seconds by filtering a Teams channel or using the search bar, you've effectively shaved time off repetitive tasks. Over days, weeks, and months, that adds up. Reflecting on these small wins can remind you why Teams is beneficial, even if you occasionally miss the familiarity of email or legacy chat apps.

Feedback in the form of colleague appreciation or comments can also be telling. Perhaps someone praises you for always uploading the latest deck in the correct channel, making it easy for them to see changes without rummaging through attachments. Or maybe they mention how tagging them directly in a post ensures they never miss a critical question. These everyday anecdotes underscore that your efforts to engage with Teams actively impact not just your workflow but also your team's overall efficiency.

If you're someone who thrives on data, you might explore whether your organization offers any usage insights or analytics. Some companies track how many active channels exist, how many messages are posted daily, or how many files are shared. While these figures often matter more to IT or management, seeing a steady uptick in channel usage or a drop in mass emails might motivate you to keep championing Teams. It reaffirms that your behavior—nudging coworkers toward channel discussions, for example—truly influences the broader culture.

Sarah's Story

Sarah had been using Teams effectively in her department for a couple of months, after conquering her own learning curve and helping a new coworker adapt. Her immediate team was generally on board—project discussions flowed through channels, quick questions went into chat, and the number of round-robin emails had dropped sharply. Yet Sarah noticed that other departments in 365 Strategies still relied heavily on email, particularly for multi-departmental projects. She often found herself included on enormous email threads that felt clumsy compared to the streamlined collaboration she enjoyed in Teams.

One day, Sarah was assigned to a cross-departmental initiative involving marketing, sales, and product. Eager to reduce friction, she created a dedicated channel and invited representatives from each department to join. Instead of funneling the project details through email attachments, she uploaded the relevant documents to that channel. She also started a pinned post summarizing the key objectives, timelines, and contact info for quick reference. In the first week, progress was slow—some participants posted in the channel, but others stuck to email or even phone calls. Sarah didn't push them too hard; she merely kept responding in the channel and gently encouraged them to place their updates there as well.

Gradually, the tide turned. The marketing lead found it convenient to drop color palettes and media assets into Teams, since she could instantly get feedback from the product manager. The sales rep appreciated how everything relevant to the initiative was pinned in one place, so if she missed a day's worth of conversation, she could scroll through the channel history. Soon, more colleagues began praising the channel's usefulness in bypassing endless "Reply All" email strings. Sarah saw a shift in attitude: people started to say, "Let me just put that in the channel," rather than, "I'll send you an email."

Buoyed by these successes, Sarah decided to share her experiences more broadly. During a monthly staff meeting, she showcased how the new cross-department channel consolidated tasks that used to be scattered in separate chat apps, emails, and personal note-taking. She pointed out how quickly the group resolved issues once everyone recognized that Teams was their primary communication hub. This public demonstration piqued interest from employees in other departments, who approached Sarah afterwards to ask for tips on setting up channels or handling persistent resisters.

While she didn't have formal analytics to prove that time was saved, Sarah felt confident that the swift feedback loops and reduced confusion spoke for themselves. She also noticed a sense of camaraderie building around the channel. When someone overcame an obstacle, they posted a quick "Here's what worked for us!" Others chimed in with supportive comments or added their own creative solutions. That sense of shared problem-solving was more dynamic than the old days of emailing static attachments.

The final sign that their approach was resonating came when a department manager from finance reached out, intrigued by Sarah's success. He wanted to replicate a similar channel-based structure for his budgeting process. Eager to help, Sarah offered quick training on how to name channels clearly, manage permissions, and tag the right people. Over the next few weeks, she watched as the finance team trickled into Teams, away from labyrinthine email chains. That momentum snowballed, and soon it felt as if entire wings of 365 Strategies had discovered the merits of pinned posts, real-time collaboration, and transparent conversation threads.

Reflecting on this evolution, Sarah recognized how a few simple actions—mentioning people in channel posts, uploading relevant files in one centralized spot, and highlighting the concrete benefits of fewer email attachments—sparked a cultural shift. Being vocal about minor victories, like cutting down a two-week email exchange into a two-day channel conversation, emboldened others to try out Teams for themselves. And as the adoption spread, employees across departments learned from each other, trading tips and cheering each other on in adopting the new platform. For Sarah, that sense of collective enthusiasm was the most rewarding outcome of all. She saw that the real payoff wasn't just in personal convenience; it was in watching an entire workplace become more cohesive, efficient, and ready to tackle collaborative challenges with confidence.

CHAPTER 8: COMPARING TEAMS TO SLACK/ZOOM

In an age where collaboration tools have become pivotal to getting work done, Microsoft Teams isn't the only platform vying for our attention. Slack and Zoom often enter the conversation as well, each offering its own take on messaging, file sharing, and video calls. Deciding which platform is "best" can feel daunting—especially if your organization uses more than one of them. This chapter aims to demystify some of the key differences among Teams, Slack, and Zoom by highlighting the core features you'll notice day to day, weighing their pros and cons, and suggesting strategies to minimize confusion if you find yourself juggling multiple collaboration tools.

Let's start with a quick rundown of what each platform is known for, focusing on the features that matter most to everyday users rather than administrative or technical details.

Slack built its reputation on real-time chat organized into channels. Slack channels function similarly to Teams channels: users create spaces for different projects, departments, or topics. But Slack's hallmark has always been a polished, intuitive chat experience, complete with emojis, GIF integrations, and robust search capabilities. While Slack supports voice and video calls, these features are often secondary compared to its rich text-based communication environment. Many organizations rely on Slack for fast-paced messaging and then switch to a different tool for formal video meetings.

Zoom, on the other hand, rose to prominence as a dedicated video conferencing solution. Its simplicity made it immensely popular: users could launch or join meetings with just a link, and the platform handled large groups and screen sharing elegantly. Zoom also features breakout rooms, webinar modes, and various advanced video settings. Although Zoom now includes a persistent chat feature, most people still think of it as the go-to platform for high-quality video calls, especially larger ones where participants may be external clients or partners.

Microsoft Teams takes a broader approach by folding chat, video calls, file sharing, and integrations with Microsoft 365 apps into one service. The channel-based system parallels Slack's approach, but Teams is deeply woven into the Office suite, so storing a file in Teams automatically tethers it to SharePoint, co-authoring a document means live editing with Word or Excel, and scheduling a meeting drops it into your Outlook calendar. This deep integration can be an advantage or an overreach, depending on your workflow. But for organizations already paying for Microsoft 365, Teams can unify multiple needs—chat, meetings, and file collaboration—under a single subscription.

The key difference you'll feel is the all-in-one nature of Teams. Slack excels in ephemeral, channel-based discussion. Zoom specializes in video calls. Teams tries to do both (plus file management, plus integrated Office apps), which can simplify your day if you need that sort of comprehensive approach. Conversely, if all you want is lightning-fast chat, Slack might feel lighter and more responsive. And if you're primarily setting up large client-facing webinars, Zoom's features for orchestrating hundreds of attendees could feel more intuitive at first.

When it comes to daily usage, each platform has a unique flavor—like different cuisines serving their own specialties. Let's break down what that might mean for you if you're doing the usual tasks: sending messages, jumping on quick calls, sharing files, and occasionally needing a bigger meeting.

Slack made a name for itself by giving teams a place to have ongoing, thread-based conversations that feel more dynamic and immediate than email. You can create public channels for transparency or private channels for sensitive discussions. People love Slack's user-friendly interface, creative reactions, and the ability to integrate with a massive array of third-party apps, from project management boards to code repositories. If your day revolves around short messages, quick polls, or an environment where a sense of fun and spontaneity is valued, Slack might feel comfortable and inviting.

However, Slack's reliance on external integrations for things like file storage or robust video conferencing can also be a downside. If your organization doesn't have a well-planned structure for these integrations, you might end up using Google Drive or Box for file sharing, Zoom for calls, and a separate calendar tool for scheduling. This can lead to "tool sprawl," where you're constantly switching from one platform to another. Slack also caps message history on its free tier, meaning conversations eventually vanish unless your company pays for a plan. This might be okay for a small startup but can pose challenges in a bigger environment that values historical knowledge.

Zoom excels at video. Joining a meeting is typically as simple as clicking a link, and you can host large sessions with hundreds or even thousands of participants in webinar mode. Many users appreciate Zoom's ease of use, stable performance even in bandwidth-challenged scenarios, and features like breakout rooms for small-group discussions. Zoom also introduced robust security measures, such as waiting rooms and passcodes, to address earlier concerns about unauthorized meeting "visitors."

Yet for everyday text-based communication or file sharing, Zoom isn't designed to be an all-in-one solution. It does have an in-meeting chat and a persistent chat feature outside of meetings, but these are nowhere near as sophisticated as Slack's or Teams' channel systems. If you rely heavily on formal presentations or hosting external guests, Zoom might be your top choice. But for ongoing project discussions or storing team documents, you'd still need a separate environment. That means you might find yourself re-inviting the same colleagues into different tools throughout the day.

For many organizations, the biggest draw of Microsoft Teams is its integration with the Microsoft 365 suite. If you're already using Outlook for email, OneDrive for file storage, and Excel or Word for documents, Teams feels like an extension that ties all these elements together. Need to draft a document collaboratively? You can embed Word inside a Teams channel so everyone can edit in real time. Planning a meeting? The Teams Calendar syncs directly to your Outlook schedule. These seamless connections reduce the friction of toggling between multiple apps.

That said, Teams' comprehensiveness can sometimes feel overwhelming. The interface is more complex than Slack's stripped-down chat or Zoom's single-purpose calls. Some users might only scratch the surface of Teams if they're not well trained, leading to confusion about how to store files or when to post in a channel vs. a chat. Additionally, if you have a slow internet connection, Teams might feel heavier due to the many features it's loading in the background. Overall, though, it excels in giving end users a unified workspace where they can chat, call, schedule, and collaborate on documents without leaving the platform.

If you're in an organization that uses multiple collaboration tools, the question of "Which one do I use for this task?" can become a daily riddle. The answer often depends on your role and the nature of your projects. Here are some thought processes that might guide you:

- Are you a heavy user of Microsoft Word, Excel, or PowerPoint, constantly referencing shared documents with your team? Then Teams likely gives you the smoothest workflow, because everything ties directly to those apps.

- Do you prefer quick, casual exchanges with colleagues, or do you work in a creative environment that values fun reactions, custom emojis, and a lively chat culture? Slack might feel more natural, especially if your tasks lean heavily on real-time discussion rather than structured file collaboration.

- Are you primarily hosting large video webinars or frequent external calls? Zoom's robust video conferencing feature set might be the easiest path, especially if you're dealing with large external audiences who just want to click a link and join.

Often, your company's official guidelines or licensing arrangements also dictate usage. If your workplace has invested heavily in Microsoft 365, it might steer you toward Teams. If your department historically used Slack or Zoom prior to a corporate transition, you might still find some holdovers reluctant to let go. In such scenarios, your best move is to minimize duplication by aligning tasks with each tool's strength. For example, continue using Zoom for company-wide town halls but push day-to-day text-based discussions into Teams channels, where they can remain organized and easily searchable.

Confusion arises when employees keep separate conversations about the same project in multiple platforms. Imagine having a Slack channel about a marketing campaign, a Teams channel with the same content, and a Zoom link for standup meetings. That fragmentation can hamper collaboration instead of improving it. If you notice such overlap, try to unify your teammates around a single "home" for textual discussions— perhaps Slack if your entire department is comfortable with it, or Teams if you need integrated file storage. Then use Zoom only for the big meetings that require advanced webinar tools. By clarifying these boundaries, you reduce the chance of missing crucial updates buried in another app.

Sarah's Story

One day, Sarah's manager approached her with a request: he wanted a short, practical comparison between Slack, Zoom, and Microsoft Teams from the perspective of everyday tasks. A corporate partner had invited 365 Strategies to collaborate in Slack, and some teams were still using Zoom for external client calls. The manager wondered if they should standardize on one platform or keep a hybrid approach.

Sarah decided to spend a week immersing herself in Slack and Zoom for her routine activities. She joined the Slack workspace her partner had set up, exploring how channels worked compared to Teams. She immediately noticed Slack's polished user interface and quick loading times. Threaded conversations made sense, but she also realized that file sharing in Slack typically involved linking Google Drive or attaching files directly, which felt less integrated than using SharePoint in Teams. She missed being able to open a Word document and co-author with colleagues in real time, a feature she'd grown fond of in Teams.

Zoom proved simple to use for scheduled and ad-hoc video calls. Sarah appreciated the crisp audio quality, and the breakout rooms were intuitive. But once the meeting ended, she had no persistent "Zoom channel" to consult for next steps, nor could she easily reference the chat thread from a previous call without saving a separate transcript. She found herself returning to Teams or email to follow up on tasks that emerged from the Zoom meeting. That extra step felt a bit cumbersome, although it wasn't insurmountable.

By contrast, Sarah realized how deeply she relied on Teams' integration with Word and Excel. When she needed to share an updated budget file, she simply uploaded it to a channel, where everyone could open it in Excel Online. Changes and comments appeared immediately. She also found that scheduling a quick internal call in Teams was straightforward; the invite synced to Outlook and the channel, providing a single place for notes, a recording, or related links.

Sarah wrote up her findings, pointing out that Slack's chat might feel sleeker and Zoom's video calls might handle large external meetings better. But for everyday usage—particularly for employees who frequently co-authored Office documents—Teams saved time and avoided the back-and-forth of switching tools. She highlighted a small anecdote: earlier that week, she'd updated a marketing plan in Word and pinned it in the channel. Her teammates opened the document right there, added suggestions, and they collectively finished the edits in under an hour. Had she tried the same in Slack or Zoom, she would have needed a separate doc-sharing platform or email attachments, creating more friction.

Encouraged by Sarah's perspective, her manager decided to keep Zoom on hand for major webinars or public-facing sessions but encouraged the staff to use Teams as their primary space for collaboration and internal meetings. For the occasional Slack-based collaborations with partners, employees would continue to adapt, but Sarah's manager asked her to create a short "Do's and Don'ts" guide for storing official company files outside the Microsoft 365 ecosystem. That way, they could maintain consistency around official documents and ensure compliance rules were met.

Reflecting on the process, Sarah found it enlightening to see how small interface quirks or missing integrations could shape how people worked. She learned to appreciate Slack's swift messaging culture but also recognized how vital Teams' all-in-one design was for tasks like file co-authoring, scheduling, and archiving conversations. In the end, she concluded that no single tool held a monopoly on excellence; each excelled in specific contexts. But for day-to-day synergy at 365 Strategies—where Office documents, channel discussions, and quick calls formed the heart of teamwork—Teams remained her top choice. She saw it not as an absolute better or worse tool than Slack or Zoom, but as the best fit for the integrated workflows she and her coworkers relied on every day.

CHAPTER 9: REAL-WORLD SUCCESS STORIES

Seeing how Microsoft Teams actually works in different real-world settings can transform an abstract tool into something that feels tangible and relevant. Sometimes, the greatest lessons come from hearing about the everyday experiences of small startups, mid-sized departments juggling multiple projects, and employees inside massive enterprises coping with large-scale rollouts. This chapter focuses on success stories that highlight how ordinary users overcame obstacles, streamlined their tasks, and ultimately found that Teams made their work lives easier. Along the way, we'll examine pitfalls to watch out for, as well as best practices that can help anyone integrate Teams more effectively into their daily routine.

Many small organizations have just a handful of employees wearing multiple hats. In these environments, every moment counts. One such startup, a design and marketing boutique with fewer than ten staff members, discovered that communication quickly became chaotic as they took on more clients. Emails and text messages flew back and forth at all hours, while files ended up in multiple cloud drives without any consistent structure. A new project manager joined the team and suggested using Microsoft Teams to consolidate their daily workflows. Initially, some staff worried that introducing a formal platform might stifle the friendly, casual vibe they enjoyed.

Yet when they gave Teams a chance, they found it surprisingly natural. They created a single Team for the entire company, dividing their work into three primary channels: "Client Projects," "Internal Brainstorm," and "General." This straightforward structure allowed them to focus on relevant discussions without building out too many channels that would go unused. Their lead designer posted mockups in the "Client Projects" channel, inviting the rest of the team to comment in real time. This was a welcome change from scrolling through long email threads or rummaging around multiple shared folders for the correct file version. If something needed quick discussion, a video call was just a click away— no more hunting for a separate conferencing tool or sending meeting links.

One of the biggest benefits they observed was the way Teams automatically saved chat histories and files in one place. Previously, if they needed to locate a specific design iteration from three months ago, someone would have to dig through a shared drive or find the right email attachment. Now, the files and the conversation around them were both accessible in the same channel. The entire group felt that they reclaimed hours each week, simply because they didn't have to constantly cross-reference messages or guess which file was the latest. The startup also discovered that having direct integration with Word and PowerPoint boosted their professionalism. When preparing a pitch deck for a client, they could co-author the slides in real time within Teams, seeing each other's edits instantly.

What sealed the deal was the realization that the app's user-friendly nature didn't erode their close-knit culture. Instead, it gave them an even better handle on who was working on what. If someone had to step away or work remotely, the rest of the team could see updates in a single feed. And while they might still text each other socially, using Teams for official business prevented messages from getting lost in a personal chat thread or overlooked until the next morning. For this tiny agency, embracing Teams was less about formalizing communication and more about making their daily hustle less chaotic.

In a larger departmental context, Teams can tackle a different set of challenges. One mid-sized marketing department within a regional bank had around 60 employees, split into multiple sub-teams handling everything from digital campaigns to event planning. They were drowning in email threads, especially when collaborating on multi-channel advertising projects. People complained about not knowing if a file was final or draft, or if a particular email thread included everyone who needed the information.

When the bank adopted Microsoft Teams organization-wide, the marketing department leaned in by structuring channels around their major campaigns and sub-teams. They created a dedicated channel for each active campaign, ensuring that all discussions, timelines, and files lived in one place. A separate channel named "Marketing Resources" served as a central library for frequently used logos, style guides, and brand guidelines. This proved invaluable, since new hires or cross-departmental collaborators could quickly find official assets without emailing multiple people for the correct file.

Meetings took on a more purposeful shape too. Instead of scheduling every brainstorming session in a separate conferencing tool, the marketing staff used Teams' built-in meeting functionality. After the call, recordings and follow-up notes automatically landed in the same channel, saving them the trouble of emailing out summaries. The pinned files feature helped them reduce the clutter of version after version of creative assets. By pinning the most current design at the top of the channel, no one had to ask, "Which version are we looking at?" or worry that a colleague was revising an outdated copy.

Perhaps the biggest transformation came from a subtle shift in how the department tracked tasks. Some sub-teams integrated Microsoft Planner into their channel tabs, assigning tasks and due dates where everyone could see them, rather than burying them in project management software that most employees rarely opened. This new transparency let people easily check which tasks were pending and who was responsible, cutting down status meetings. The result was fewer over-scheduled hours for everyone, as many routine updates and clarifications took place asynchronously in Teams.

While not everyone embraced the switch immediately—some older employees still preferred firing off emails for certain requests—the overall feedback was positive. Fewer missed deadlines and a more coherent record of campaign progress emerged as clear wins. Over time, many who had initially resisted grew to appreciate the ability to glance through channel histories to catch up on developments, rather than searching through an inbox full of messages with cryptic subject lines.

Scaling Teams in an enterprise setting often presents a monumental challenge. One global manufacturing firm, spanning thousands of employees across multiple continents, decided to standardize on Microsoft Teams after years of using disparate apps. Instead of every regional office choosing its own collaboration tool, leadership wanted a single platform that integrated with their Microsoft 365 investment. The shift was announced company-wide, and employees were given a grace period to migrate ongoing discussions and files into Teams.

The early phase was somewhat chaotic. Channels popped up everywhere, often duplicating the same topic under slightly different names. Employees in Asia might create a "Product Launch – Q3" channel, while their North American counterparts created "Q3 Product Launch," splitting conversations about the same project into two locations. Many individuals found themselves uncertain about which channel or team to post in.

The turning point came when a task force of "Team Champions"— people from different departments who had shown a knack for adopting Teams effectively—began cleaning up and consolidating the sprawl. They guided coworkers to unify naming conventions and pinned essential instructions in a general "Teams Best Practices" channel. Over a few months, the chaos subsided. Users reported that once they knew which channels to visit for product updates or finance approvals, their daily tasks became smoother than before.

Even in this large-scale rollout, the intangible benefits loomed large. People who regularly traveled for work no longer missed urgent updates because everything was accessible via Teams on their phones. Historical chat logs allowed newcomers to glean essential background without scheduling multiple catch-up meetings. And cross-regional projects, which had previously stumbled over time zones and email delays, found a new rhythm by using channels dedicated to real-time or near-real-time discussion.

Enterprise employees often mention one critical pitfall: channel overload. With thousands of staff members, it's all too easy for channels to balloon, making it tough for any one person to stay organized. This leads some employees to mute many channels, risking missed updates. Yet the solution typically lies in thoughtful governance and personal management of notifications. Once a healthy channel structure emerges—coupled with employees taking the time to pin or favorite the channels that matter most—people say they can navigate the ocean of conversations more confidently than they ever did with global email chains.

Across these diverse stories—startups, mid-sized teams, and enterprises—a few key themes emerge that can help any single user thrive in Microsoft Teams.

One pitfall is channel overload. It's tempting to create new channels for every subtopic, but that can dilute attention. A mindful approach is to create channels only for distinct, ongoing conversations, and avoid duplication. If you see multiple channels covering the same theme, consider merging them before confusion sets in.

Forgetting to mention people is another stumbling block. If you want a colleague to see your message, tagging them using "@Name" ensures they receive a notification. Otherwise, messages in active channels can slip by unnoticed, especially in large organizations. That's where pinned posts and pinned files become crucial: they direct everyone to the most important information or resources without requiring repeated explanations.

Another lesson is to rely on the integrated file management rather than defaulting to email attachments or separate cloud drives. Storing key documents in a channel ensures that updates, comments, and older versions remain connected to the relevant conversation. This is particularly helpful in larger groups where members join mid-project and need to get up to speed.

Users who adopt a balanced approach to notifications also tend to have better experiences. Setting channel-specific or mention-based alerts can help you stay informed about the topics that matter while avoiding the exhaustion of constant pings. Some employees also set "Quiet Hours" on their mobile app, preserving their personal time outside work.

Finally, consistent real-time collaboration fosters a sense of shared ownership. Whether it's a startup creating a collaborative brand style guide, a mid-sized department hashing out a marketing plan, or an enterprise team launching a multinational project, real success stories pivot around the idea that Teams is more than just a replacement for email—it's a platform that centralizes knowledge, encourages transparency, and frees employees from the quagmire of scattered information.

Sarah's Story

After months of actively using Teams at 365 Strategies, Sarah began to notice how various pockets of the company had started leveraging the platform. Intrigued, she decided to conduct a few quick "listening" sessions, chatting informally with coworkers in different departments about their experiences. Her aim was to piece together a broader picture of how Teams had impacted everyday workloads and gather insights she could share with the rest of the organization.

She discovered, for instance, that a small analytics group in her office used to struggle with version control on Excel sheets. Before Teams, the group members sometimes found themselves editing different local copies, merging changes via email attachments, and risking data inconsistencies. Once they moved to storing the master Excel file in a dedicated channel, they co-authored the same file simultaneously. The next time Sarah spoke to them, they were almost giddy about no longer having to guess who had the latest draft—Teams handled the versioning behind the scenes.

In another department, the HR team recounted how they once spent ages scheduling candidate interviews via email. By creating a private channel for interview logistics and tying it to a shared calendar in Teams, they cut the scheduling back-and-forth nearly in half. Candidates received invites faster, and the internal team saw, at a glance, which recruiter was assigned to which role. This smaller improvement, though not earth-shattering, meant less confusion and fewer missed appointments.

Perhaps the most striking testimonial came from someone in the sales department. She told Sarah how large-scale deals previously required assembling multiple PDF contracts, approval forms, and lengthy email strings among different internal stakeholders. Now, a sales channel served as a single repository for all relevant documents. When a new deal popped up, the assigned rep pinned the contract draft, tagged the legal representative, and hosted a short call to finalize terms. She called it "a one-stop shop for signing six-figure contracts," which made her job feel more cohesive and less scattered than before.

Sarah condensed these stories into a short presentation, interspersing quotes from each department. During a casual lunch-and-learn session, she shared these success tales with colleagues, who'd sometimes been aware only of their own small wins. Seeing how Teams was applied across such varied tasks—data analysis, recruiting, sales deals—opened everyone's eyes to the platform's flexibility. And by showing how small teams overcame common pitfalls (like chaotic file sharing or scheduling headaches), Sarah provided practical guidance others could adapt.

Reflecting on what she'd learned, Sarah felt more convinced than ever that Teams thrived on user engagement. It wasn't enough for IT to roll out the software and hope for the best. Real progress happened because individuals—like the analytics group or the HR team—took ownership of their workflows and experimented with what Teams could do. They discovered minor but impactful tricks along the way, whether it was co-authoring an Excel file or organizing interviews in a private channel. Each success story underscored that it wasn't the technology alone that made a difference; it was how people used it to reshape their daily practices.

As Sarah left the lunch-and-learn, a coworker from the finance department cornered her, asking if she had suggestions for cleaning up a messy set of channels. Smiling, Sarah offered to walk through channel consolidation and pinned posts, reminding them to keep a careful eye on naming conventions. She realized that while every success story was unique, they all showed how an organized approach to Teams, combined with genuine buy-in from the team, spelled the difference between frustration and productivity.

By the end of that day, Sarah had compiled enough anecdotes to fill an internal newsletter, further spreading the message about how everyday employees were harnessing Teams. That synergy, from small teams to large enterprise settings, convinced Sarah that the key to unlocking Teams' full potential lay in people sharing their experiences, learning from each other's triumphs and missteps, and steadily evolving how they collaborated—together.

CHAPTER 10: LOOKING AHEAD— CONTINUAL LEARNING AND FEATURE EVOLUTION

By this point, you've seen how Microsoft Teams can transform day-to-day communication, enhance file-sharing workflows, and bring coworkers together across departments and even continents. But unlike tools of the past that stayed static once installed, Teams continues to evolve at a rapid pace. New features appear regularly, integrations expand, and artificial intelligence begins to play a larger role. The journey with Teams is never truly "complete," because the platform itself keeps adapting in response to user feedback and shifting technology trends.

Learning how to embrace this state of constant change can help you and your colleagues remain agile. In this final chapter, we'll explore why Teams is an ever-evolving service, discuss how end users can stay ahead of the curve without getting overwhelmed, and propose ways to keep enthusiasm high—even months or years after the initial rollout. We'll then conclude with a final glimpse into Sarah's story, as she experiences firsthand how new features spark fresh ideas and a renewed sense of excitement around collaboration.

One of the defining characteristics of Microsoft Teams is that it lives in the cloud. This cloud-first approach allows Microsoft to roll out updates and enhancements continuously, rather than forcing users to wait for a single large upgrade every year or two. As a result, your Teams interface might look subtly different from one month to the next. Sometimes, a new icon appears or a menu layout shifts. Other times, you might discover entire new functionalities, such as additional meeting controls, advanced channel settings, or AI-driven features that summarize conversations.

The introduction of AI into Teams reflects how modern collaboration tools are moving beyond simple text chat and file sharing. Copilot, for instance, is Microsoft's vision of an AI assistant that can help gather insights from large conversation threads, automatically draft summaries, or suggest tasks based on context clues. For an end user, this might mean you ask Copilot, "Please give me a summary of our last channel discussion regarding Q4 budgets," and it presents key points within seconds. Or perhaps the AI flags an upcoming due date it finds in a conversation thread, prompting you to add a task in Planner. While these capabilities are still evolving, they hint at a future where the lines between manual collaboration and automated assistance become increasingly blurred.

Beyond AI, Teams regularly expands its ecosystem of integrations. One month, you might see that a popular project management tool has released a deeper tie-in with Teams, allowing you to create tasks or follow updates directly within a channel. Another month, you might learn about improvements to the Teams mobile app that streamline how notifications appear on your phone. Because Teams is part of the broader Microsoft 365 environment, it also benefits from innovations in Word, Excel, OneDrive, SharePoint, and Power Platform apps like Power Automate or Power BI. Each update can cascade into new ways of working, especially if you remain curious enough to try them out.

The key is to remember that the pace of these changes can vary. Some months might bring only minor bug fixes or visual tweaks, while other months deliver headline-grabbing announcements. That's why it helps to keep an eye on official release notes or in-app announcements. Microsoft often shares upcoming features on its public roadmap, giving you a sneak peek of what might arrive soon. If your organization has an admin portal, the IT team may post messages about upcoming changes and the potential impact on your daily routines. Staying informed can prevent surprises—like suddenly seeing a new layout for your chat list—and position you to make the most of any improvements as soon as they appear.

Continual learning is the cornerstone of thriving in a platform that updates itself on a regular basis. While official training sessions might happen only during the initial rollout or at designated company events, there are many ways to keep your skills sharp. Some employees form small study groups or champion circles, meeting once a month to discuss new features or lesser-known capabilities. Others find value in self-directed exploration: setting aside a few minutes each week to click through menus they haven't used or to explore the official Microsoft Teams blog posts that detail newly launched functionalities.

When Teams announces something like breakout rooms for large meetings or reorganized channel layouts, it may be tempting to revert to the older methods you already know. But trying out these additions can open up new efficiencies. Maybe your team has always found large calls unwieldy, with participants talking over each other. By testing breakout rooms, you could discover a more structured approach to brainstorming, letting smaller groups tackle subtopics and then rejoin the main session to consolidate ideas. Similarly, if you notice a new "pinned replies" feature in channel conversations, playing around with it could reveal a simple way to highlight essential posts without them getting lost in the scroll of daily chatter.

Encouraging your colleagues to do the same—whether through informal Slack-style channels or scheduled "Teams Tips" meetups—ensures that the entire department evolves alongside the tool. You might find that once a few brave souls experiment with a fresh integration or a refined layout, others are more willing to follow. The payoff is that your organization avoids stagnating and remains open to ways that Teams can solve everyday problems. In this way, "training" becomes an ongoing, dynamic process, rather than a one-off event that everyone forgets a week later.

Six months or a year after adopting Teams, many workplaces risk falling into a rut. Some of the initial excitement fades, people settle into routines, and fewer employees feel the drive to keep exploring new features. That's where small, consistent efforts to maintain enthusiasm can make a difference.

One effective approach is to hold mini "new feature" demos every month or quarter. This doesn't have to be a formal event. You could simply devote the first five or ten minutes of a regular team meeting to highlight any relevant updates in Teams. Did Microsoft improve the search function? Show it off. Did your org enable a new file-sharing option or a built-in poll for meetings? Demonstrate a quick example. By regularly showcasing these incremental changes, you remind everyone that Teams is evolving and that there may be new shortcuts to make their work easier.

Another way to sustain interest is to invite employees to share collaborative tips in an open channel. If someone figures out a neat trick—like how to link tasks in Planner to a chat thread or how to embed a custom app—they can post a short explanation or record a brief screencast. Over time, this channel becomes an internal knowledge base of user-discovered best practices. The effect is cumulative: the more your colleagues see that the organization values peer-to-peer learning, the more they'll volunteer their own tips, spurring a virtuous cycle of continuous improvement.

Some companies also encourage friendly competitions around Teams usage. For example, a department might set a goal to cut internal email volume by a certain percentage, or to reduce the length of recurring status meetings by moving routine updates into channels. Celebrating these achievements—perhaps by recognizing employees who contributed the most ideas or saw the biggest gains—keeps the momentum alive. Recognition doesn't have to be grand; a simple shout-out in the "All-Hands" channel or a small reward can suffice. By framing changes in daily work habits as a collective victory, you maintain positivity around the evolving platform.

Ultimately, maintaining enthusiasm comes down to reinforcing the narrative that Teams is not static software. Just as your business evolves in response to market conditions, your collaboration platform also evolves in response to user needs, new technologies, and ongoing feedback from millions of people worldwide. The trick is not to view each update as an inconvenience, but as an opportunity to refine how you and your team operate.

Sarah's Story

Several months after Sarah led her department's successful shift to Teams, she found herself browsing her Outlook calendar for interesting internal events. A Microsoft Ignite session was happening virtually, promising sneak peeks at upcoming Teams features and improvements to the Microsoft 365 ecosystem. Intrigued by the mention of AI-driven meeting summaries and advanced security enhancements, she decided to attend.

The Ignite keynote left her impressed but slightly overwhelmed. She learned that Copilot, the AI assistant rumored to be in development, was moving beyond concept into pilot programs. The demonstration showed how you could ask Copilot to create a bulleted summary of a day's worth of channel chatter or propose action items from a recorded meeting. Sarah imagined this freeing her from the tedious task of sifting through older threads, especially when a manager asked for a quick recap. She also saw a preview of new advanced meeting layouts, letting hosts rearrange participants in more flexible ways, and heard about deeper integrations with popular third-party apps.

Rather than just passively absorbing this information, Sarah made a few notes on potential ways these features could help 365 Strategies. The next morning, she logged into Teams and created a new post in the "Technology Updates" channel, summarizing what she'd seen. She described how Copilot's summarization could save team leads time, how meeting layout improvements might address the department's desire for more interactive video calls, and how upcoming security controls could offer peace of mind to colleagues in finance or legal roles. She ended her post by inviting anyone curious to ping her for more details.

To her surprise, the channel lit up with conversation. Coworkers asked if certain features would be behind higher license tiers or how the AI would handle sensitive data. Others wondered if the advanced meeting layouts would simplify their large monthly reviews with external vendors. A manager from another department suggested they run a short pilot session once the features became available. Sarah found the back-and-forth refreshing. It reminded her that adopting new technology is a shared process, where every user can contribute ideas for how best to weave these tools into everyday tasks.

Over the following weeks, Sarah compiled more information from Microsoft's documentation, including best guesses on release timelines for the features teased at Ignite. She felt energized by the prospect of helping her colleagues integrate novel functionalities. It wasn't just about personal curiosity anymore; it was about leading her department into the future, ensuring they didn't stagnate in the face of rapid change.

Reflecting on her journey, Sarah recognized that the process of continual learning and adaptation was nearly as important as the platform's core features themselves. She'd started as a slightly overwhelmed new hire grappling with Teams basics, and now she was seen as a "user-level champion"—someone with enough experience and enthusiasm to guide others. That shift, she realized, stemmed from her willingness to keep exploring and to share what she discovered, rather than waiting for formal directives or ignoring updates that seemed daunting.

As she walked out of a brainstorming session with her manager—this time focusing on how AI might help track action items across multiple channels—Sarah smiled at the thought of how far she and the rest of 365 Strategies had come. Teams would never be "done," but that was precisely the point. By staying curious, adapting to new features, and encouraging coworkers to do the same, Sarah felt confident that Teams would remain a reliable, evolving partner in their collective work. The final lesson she carried away was that any platform is only as valuable as the mindset of the people using it, and in a world that changes constantly, a culture of continuous improvement trumps a one-time rollout every single time.

YOUR ONGOING JOURNEY WITH MICROSOFT TEAMS

As you reach the end of this guide, you've likely discovered that Microsoft Teams is far more than just an application you log into each morning. It's a dynamic environment—constantly improving, continuously introducing new integrations, and capable of reshaping how your entire organization handles communication and collaboration. The ten chapters you've explored have examined Teams from multiple angles, addressing topics such as how to shift away from email over-reliance, how to create effective channels and manage guest access, and how to keep your work secure without stifling the very flexibility that makes Teams so appealing.

Over the course of this book, you've seen how Teams can streamline routine tasks—like file sharing, team announcements, and daily stand-ups—by centralizing them in one convenient interface. You've explored why certain administrative details (like licensing tiers) still matter in that they inform which features you can expect to see. You've also seen how data residency and compliance, though sometimes invisible on the surface, have real implications for where and how you store information.

Crucially, you've read about how your own actions—whether you're adding a new coworker to a channel, choosing to share files in Teams rather than emailing attachments, or scheduling ad-hoc video calls—can drive broader organizational change. Even if your official title isn't "IT administrator" or "Team Owner," you play a key role in shaping how your colleagues perceive and adopt Teams. Small gestures, like tagging people with @mentions or pinning frequently used resources, can prompt others to do the same, gradually building a culture where Teams becomes a trusted, familiar tool.

You've also encountered scenarios for different organizational sizes, from small startups with fewer than ten people to sprawling enterprises handling global rollouts. The common thread in these stories is that Teams—when used thoughtfully—bridges gaps between departments, mitigates confusion over file versions, and accelerates the process of decision-making. But the journey doesn't end after you've mastered the basics. Indeed, as this book has reiterated, Microsoft continually evolves Teams with new features and integrations. Each update can introduce fresh possibilities—or new complexities.

Throughout this guide, a handful of core ideas have recurred, tying many of the chapters together:

1. **Transparency and Openness**
   Teams channels and group chats encourage open sharing of information. Rather than archiving crucial details in an inbox that only a few people can see, teams post discussions, files, and updates in a space the entire group can access. This eliminates the "I wasn't copied on that email" problem and reduces the friction of distributing essential resources.

2. **Organization and Personalization**
   While Teams can be a powerful all-in-one platform, it can also feel overwhelming if you're not intentional about how you organize channels, manage notifications, or store files. The best experiences often come from users who customize their environment—pinning channels that matter, adjusting notifications to avoid overload, and labeling or tagging documents clearly. Spending a bit of effort on tidiness pays off in the long run, making it easier to find information and keep track of tasks.

3. **Collaboration and Co-Authoring**
   From the earliest chapters, you've learned how Teams integrates with Word, Excel, PowerPoint, and other Microsoft 365 applications, letting multiple people edit a file in real time. This approach dramatically reduces version-control headaches, fosters quicker feedback loops, and centralizes the conversation around a given document or deck. The shift from emailing drafts back

70

and forth to co-authoring in a single shared location can be a defining moment for many teams transitioning into more streamlined digital workflows.

4. **Security and Compliance**
   While day-to-day users may not be configuring advanced tenant settings, everyone has a role in ensuring sensitive files go to the right channels and that external guests see only what they need to see. Small steps—like confirming a channel's privacy level or storing regulated data in a restricted team—can protect both you and your organization from potential mishaps. Awareness and caution, especially when inviting guests or uploading documents, help preserve trust and maintain compliance with laws or corporate policies.

5. **Ongoing Learning and Adaptation**
   Possibly the most important overarching theme is that learning Teams is not a one-time task. By its nature, Teams is iterative: features get refined, new capabilities appear, and user preferences evolve. The more open you are to exploring updates, the better you'll adapt and the more likely you are to discover shortcuts or solutions that save time. Sharing these discoveries with colleagues can ignite a broader sense of curiosity and engagement.

If you're feeling confident with the essentials, consider leveling up your Teams usage in a few key areas:

- **Experiment with Integrations**: If your role involves project management, explore apps like Planner or Trello inside Teams. If you rely heavily on analytics, investigate how Power BI dashboards can be embedded in a channel for real-time data visibility.

- **Refine Your Meeting Practices**: Try advanced meeting features, like breakout rooms, meeting polls, or live transcription, to make virtual sessions more interactive and inclusive.

- **Guide New Hires**: Turn your knowledge into a resource for newcomers, the way Sarah did in her stories. Draft a quick "Getting Started" channel post or create an informal buddy system.

- **Monitor Microsoft's Roadmap**: Keep an eye on announcements in your Microsoft 365 admin center or watch for blog posts about Teams updates. Even if you're not an admin, a simple awareness of what's coming can spark conversations and inspire you to test new features as they roll out.

You might also want to exchange tips with colleagues who've delved into specialized scenarios, like setting up phone queues in Teams or implementing advanced security policies. Even if you don't need those features daily, understanding their value can strengthen your role as a resourceful, adaptable team member.

While technology like Teams can undeniably reshape workflows, it's ultimately your team's culture—your willingness to share knowledge openly, to experiment with new tools, and to continuously refine processes—that determines success. If your organization adopts a mindset of "we've always done it this way," no platform will fulfill its potential. Conversely, if you remain open to incremental improvements and encourage your peers to do the same, Teams can serve as a living ecosystem where files are never lost, conversations remain transparent, and tasks move from idea to execution with minimal friction.

In short, Teams is a mirror reflecting your collective approach to collaboration. Use it haphazardly, and it can become cluttered—just another source of digital noise. Use it intentionally, and it becomes a catalyst for clearer communication, more streamlined processes, and a tangible sense of unity, whether you're working together in the same office or from different corners of the globe.

A Final Look at Sarah's Journey

Sarah's story began as that of a relatively new employee feeling drowned by email threads and uncertain about how Teams might help. Over the chapters, she learned to post weekly updates in a channel instead of drafting mass emails, discovered how to manage notifications so she wasn't overwhelmed, and even introduced new hires to the platform's fundamentals. As her confidence grew, she took on a more proactive role—setting up channels for cross-departmental collaboration, demonstrating advanced features to skeptical colleagues, and eventually attending Microsoft's webinars to catch a glimpse of upcoming enhancements.

Her experiences illustrate that any ordinary user—someone who doesn't hold an official IT title—can become a catalyst for positive transformation. By consistently showing how Teams simplified her tasks, Sarah gained informal credibility. Coworkers found her approachable, asked her for tips, and began adopting the practices she modeled. Bit by bit, entire workflows shifted. Inbox clutter declined, transparency improved, and even large-scale projects benefited from having a singular space for communication and file management.

Now, as Microsoft continues to refine Teams, Sarah isn't caught off guard. She expects the platform to keep evolving. Rather than resist new features, she sees them as opportunities to iterate on her own routines. Whenever an improvement arrives—like AI-based meeting summaries or more flexible channel management—she's among the first to experiment and share her findings. This cyclical process of learning and teaching underscores that in a tool as dynamic as Teams, no one ever truly "masters" everything. Instead, we keep growing, discovering fresh ways to collaborate, and embracing the idea that the future of work is shaped by our willingness to adapt.

Sarah's journey can be yours, too. Whether you're just starting out or already feel comfortable in Teams, each day offers a chance to refine your habits, help a coworker tackle a new feature, or propose a small change in channel structure that benefits everyone. By combining practical knowledge with a spirit of exploration, you become a driving force behind how your organization uses Teams—and, more importantly, how it evolves a culture of effective, forward-thinking teamwork.